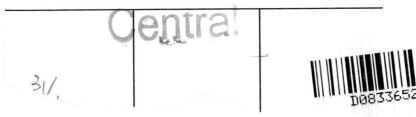

THE History OF Christmas

Helen Cox Cannons

raintree

a Capstone company — publishers for children

Raintree is an imprint of Capstone Global Library Limited, a company incorporated in England and Wales having its registered office at 264 Banbury Road, Oxford, OX2 7DY – Registered company number: 6695582

www.raintree.co.uk
myorders@raintree.co.uk

Text © Capstone Global Library Limited 2019

The moral rights of the proprietor have been asserted.

Edited by Clare Lewis
Designed by Terri Poburka
Original illustrations © Capstone Global Library Limited 2018
Picture research by Jo Miller
Production by Tori Abraham
Originated by Capstone Global Library Ltd
Printed and bound in India

ISBN 978 1 4747 6218 2
22 21 20 19 18
10 9 8 7 6 5 4 3 2 1

British Library Cataloguing in Publication Data
A full catalogue record for this book is available from the British Library.

Acknowledgements
We would like to thank the following for permission to reproduce photographs:

Image Credits
Alamy: Chronical, 20, (right); Bridgeman Images: SZ Photo/Scheri, 8, (top); Getty Images: Anadolu Agency/Contributor, 22, (left), Bettmann/Contributor, 18, Caiaimage/Robert Daly, 19, Fine Art Photographic/Contributor, 10, GraphicaArtis/Contributor, 20, (left), Hulton Archive/Stringer, 17, Library of Congress/Contributor, 11; iStockphoto: Andrew_Howe, 7, SolStock, 5; Shutterstock: BBA Photography, 6, DGLimages, 8, (bottom), Halfpoint, 9, Lucky Business, 4, Matthew J Thomas, 21, Mirelle, 22, (right), Oleg Golovnev, 14, POPKOV ALEKSANDR, 12, Vector Tradition SM, cover; Wikimedia: Allan Ramsay, 16, Sir Henry Cole, 15, The Yorck Project: 10.000 Meisterwerke der Malerei. DVD-ROM, 2002. ISBN 3936122202. Distributed by DIRECTMEDIA Publishing GmbH., 13

Design Elements
Shutterstock: Vector Tradition SM

Every effort has been made to contact copyright holders of material reproduced in this book. Any omissions will be rectified in subsequent printings if notice is given to the publisher.

All the internet addresses (URLs) given in this book were valid at the time of going to press. However, due to the dynamic nature of the internet, some addresses may have changed, or sites may have changed or ceased to exist since publication. While the author and publisher regret any inconvenience this may cause readers, no responsibility for any such changes can be accepted by either the author or the publisher.

Contents

Some words are shown in bold, **like this**. You can find out what they mean by looking in the glossary.

It's Christmas Day!

It's Christmas Day! Father Christmas has been! There are presents under the Christmas tree. Everyone is excited.

Christmas Day is on 25 December. Families and loved ones get together at Christmas time. We celebrate by eating a special dinner and sharing gifts. Why do we do this?

The Christmas story

Yule log

There have been winter **festivals** for thousands of years. The Romans had important festivals in the winter.

Winter Solstice celebrations were also in late December. People looked forward to longer and warmer days. In Scandinavia and northern Europe, the Winter Solstice is known as "Yule". This is where the name for Yule logs comes from.

Two thousand years ago, **Christianity** began to spread. The Christian holy book, the Bible, tells us that a baby was born in Bethlehem. The baby's name was Jesus Christ. Wise men, shepherds and angels came to see the baby. People believed the baby was the son of God.

Nobody knows exactly when Jesus was born. But Christians linked the story of Jesus's birth with the winter festivals. They called the new festival Christmas.

Who is Father Christmas?

In **ancient** times, Father Christmas was known as "King Winter". People believed that if they left King Winter food and drink, he would visit and reward them with a mild winter. They believed he wore a green hooded cloak.

Today, people often call Father Christmas Santa Claus. The image of a jolly Santa in a red suit with a white beard was made popular by a Coca-Cola™ advert. It was created in 1931 by an **illustrator** called Haddon Sundblom.

Why do we hang out stockings?

Many people leave out stockings on Christmas Eve for Father Christmas to fill. This is because of a **legend**. The story goes that a poor man had three daughters. He had no money and was worried that his daughters would not be able to marry.

An early version of Father Christmas, called St Nicholas, was visiting the town. He heard about the poor man's troubles. St Nicholas dropped some gold coins down the man's chimney. The coins landed in his daughter's stockings that were drying by the fire.

Why do we send Christmas cards?

In the mid-1800s, a new postal system called the "Penny Post" was introduced in Britain. People could put a penny stamp on a letter and send it anywhere around the country. Sending letters became very popular, especially at Christmas time.

A MERRY CHRISTMAS
AND
A HAPPY NEW YEAR
TO YOU

Published at Summerly's Home Treasury Office.
12, Old Bond Street, London.

From

In 1843, a man called Henry Cole had an idea. He asked his artist friend, John Horsley, to design a Christmas card. The picture showed people eating and drinking. It also showed people caring for the poor. Cole had 1,000 copies printed and sold them for 1 shilling (5 pence) each. This was the very first Christmas card.

Why do we eat turkey on Christmas Day?

Goose was eaten in the Middle Ages.

Records of Christmas Day feasts go back to the **Middle Ages**. People ate goose, swan, pheasant, peacock or boar's head on Christmas Day. Turkeys were brought to Britain in the mid-1500s. They are originally from North America.

Turkey was seen as a **luxury** food up until the 1950s. Meat was **expensive**, so not everyone could afford it. Then meat became cheaper and easier to keep, because fridges were more common. Now, most families eat roast turkey on Christmas Day. Some families eat roast chicken, beef or nut roast instead.

Why do we eat Christmas pudding?

The idea of a Christmas pudding started in the 1300s. It was a porridge called "frumenty". Frumenty was made of beef and **mutton**, with raisins, currants, prunes, wines and spices. During Victorian times, plum puddings became more like the Christmas puddings we eat today. Wealthy Victorians often cooked theirs in moulds (like jelly moulds). They could be in the shape of towers or castles!

The coin placed in the Christmas pudding for luck was always a silver "sixpence". Many people still do this today, using modern coins. Sometimes people set fire to their Christmas pudding before serving it!

Christmas around the world!

Australia

South Africa

Millions of people around the world celebrate Christmas. People eat all kinds of Christmas meals, from goat curries in the Caribbean to whale **blubber** in Greenland. In countries such as Australia and South Africa, the weather in December is hot. People eat their Christmas meals on the beach!

Glossary

ancient very old; many years ago

blubber layer of fat on some animals

carol popular song or hymn played at Christmas time

Christianity religion based on the teachings of Jesus Christ

festival day or event of celebrations

illustrator person who draws or creates pictures for books or magazines

legend story that becomes well known but may not be true

luxury something special that not everyone can have

Middle Ages period in history from about 1100 to 1453

mutton meat from an adult sheep eaten as food

record write down; something that is written down

tradition belief or custom that is passed down through families

Winter Solstice shortest day of the year; in the UK, this is usually 21 December

Find out more

Christmas Around the World **series (First Facts)**,
Jack Manning & Cheryl L. Enderlein (Raintree, 2017)

The Christmas Story, Sophie Piper (Lion Children's
Books, 2016)

Index